AN ANTHOLOGY OF ENGLISH MEDIEVAL AND RENAISSANCE VOCAL MUSIC

Part songs for one to six voices

EDITED BY NOAH GREENBERG

WITH AN INTRODUCTION BY

JOEL NEWMAN

The Norton Library
W · W · NORTON & COMPANY · INC ·
NEW YORK

TO TONI

FIRST PUBLISHED IN THE NORTON LIBRARY 1968 BY ARRANGEMENT
WITH DOUBLEDAY & COMPANY, INC.

Originally published under the title *An English Song Book*

ALL RIGHTS RESERVED
PUBLISHED SIMULTANEOUSLY IN CANADA BY
GEORGE J. MC LEOD LIMITED, TORONTO
Printed in the United States of America

ISBN   0   393   00461   9

CONTENTS

INDEXES

EDITOR'S NOTE

I would like to thank Joel Newman for a considerable share in making this book; he was particularly useful in locating materials and in editorial tasks. May I also thank Walter R. Davis of the Massachusetts Institute of Technology, Dr. Jean Misrahi of Fordham, and Dr. David Goldstein for their helpful assistance.

I am grateful to the following libraries for the use of source material from their collections: The British Museum for the Henry VIII, Cornysh, and Pygott works in Add. Ms. 31922 and for original editions of Morley, Wilbye, and Weelkes; The Folger Shakespeare Library, Washington, D. C., for Byrd's *Songs of Sundrie Natures*.

Noah Greenberg

ACKNOWLEDGMENTS

Acknowledgment is hereby gratefully made to the following publishers and copyright holders for permission to reprint the selections listed below:

The American Institute of Musicology for "Alleluia psallat" from *Worcester Fragments*, published by the American Institute of Musicology, by permission of Dr. Armen Carapetyan.

Appleton-Century-Crofts, Inc., for "Angelus ad Virginem" from *Examples of Music before 1400*, edited by Harold Gleason. Copyright 1942 by F. S. Crofts & Co., Inc.

The Carnegie United Kingdom Trust for the "Gloria" from "Westron Wynde Mass," "O Lord, increase my faith," "Agnus Dei," "Salvator mundi," "Nunc dimittis," and "Emendemus in melius" from *Tudor Church Music*, published by the Oxford University Press.

The Clarendon Press, Oxford, for "Worldes blis ne last," "Edi Beo," "Jesu Cristes milde moder" from *English Lyrics of the Thirteenth Century*, ed. Carleton Brown.

Galaxy Music Corporation for "Deo Gracias Anglia," "Nowel sing we bothe al and some," and "Nova, Nova" from *Musica Britannica*, Vol. IV—*Mediaeval Carols*, copyright 1958 by The Royal Musical Association, printed by permission of The Royal Musical Association and Stainer and Bell, Ltd.

Music and Letters for "Edi beo" from Vol. XVI (1935) transcribed by Manfred Bukofzer.

The Musical Quarterly for "Alas departynge is ground of woo" from *The Musical Quarterly* for January 1942. Copyright 1942 by G. Schirmer, Inc.

W. W. Norton & Company, Inc., for "Jesu Cristes milde moder," "Beata progenies," "Crist and Sainte Marie," and "Man mei longe" from *Music in the Middle Ages*, by Gustave Reese.

The Plainsong and Mediaeval Music Society for "Sanctus" by Roy Henry from *The Old Hall Manuscript*, Vol. III.

University of California Press for "Sumer Is Icumen In" from *Sumer Is Icumen In: A Revision*, by Manfred Bukofzer.

INTRODUCTION

Reader, this is not just one more songbook to open on your piano. Rather select your best table, one without sharp edges, and load it down with good cheer, leaving place for this book. Then gather around your forces, partake, and take part. Or, since the collection begins with some lyrics from the old "monophonic" days when music and melody were one and the same, try these pieces alone after your morning coffee. Perhaps, like Sir Toby, you and your companions may want to roar out Cornysh's *Blow Thy Horne Hunter* and Ravenscroft's *New Oysters* in some wine cellar or on a country lane with a rushing wind to play hob with the parts. Muster as many melodic instruments as you can find—every rebec, viol, gittern, and lute you know of. But failing these, recorders, violins, flutes, cellos, and the like will make do splendidly. Use them to fill in for absent singing friends, or to reinforce your voices, or even, in time of chills and laryngitis, to play a piece from top to bottom as a purely instrumental project. But use the piano, the guitar, or the harpsichord only *in extremis;* these will do best if they pretend to be melodic instruments, lining out a voice part or two. Perhaps, after all, the piano can best serve as a convenient music rack.

Convivial and hearty music is here in plenty, but side by side with it is reflective, elegiac, and ritual utterance — which prompts a quick modulation to serious commentary. When as many as forty-seven compositions from so large a span of time are assembled, it may be profitable to take an overview, grouping them according to function. Nine of the works are liturgical in use, music for the service. Three belong to the Ordinary of the Roman Catholic Mass: a *Sanctus* by Henry IV, part of the *Gloria* from Taverner's *Westron Wynde* Mass, and the *Agnus Dei* from a beautiful four-part Mass by Tallis. Shorter settings of texts from the Proper or the Office, called by the all-inclusive term motets, include an *Alleluia* from Worcester, Power's sonorous *Beata progenies,* Dunstable's *Sancta Maria,* and two Elizabethan examples, the *Salvator Mundi* by Tallis for use at Compline on Christmas and Byrd's Ash Wednesday motet, *Emendemus in Melius.* After the Reformation, Mass and Office were replaced by Services and the motet gave way to the anthem. Gibbons' *O Lord, Increase My Faith* illustrates the generally simpler texture of the anthem. The *Nunc Dimittis* (Simeon's Canticle) from Tomkins' First Evensong Service exemplifies the sumptuous style of Anglican cathedral music which often demanded soloists, full choir, and instrumental support from organ and viols.

England's long-standing tradition of popular religious lyric poetry is represented by the earliest moralizing and religious songs (Nos. 1–5), by the justly famous fifteenth-century carols (Nos. 13–15), and by such part songs of piety as Byrd's *Susanna Fayre* and Ravenscroft's *O Lord, Turn Not Away* and *Remember Oh Thou Man*.

Secular compositions often fall into two classes, sophisticated works for courtly or skilled domestic music-making and "popular," middle-class music. The high-art genre is well represented here by the poignant *Alas Departynge*, the part songs of Henry VIII's circle (Nos. 16–20), and a large group of Elizabethan madrigals, canzonets, and ayres (Nos. 24, 26–38). Good sources of popular Elizabethan part song are the Ravenscroft collections, *Pammelia*, *Deuteromelia*, and *Mellismata*, whose great appeal is evident from their frequent reprintings. Such lusty catches and songs are the best advertisement for the "Merrie England" aspect of Elizabethan and Jacobean life.

If the reader is willing, another quick ramble through the collection is now proposed, this time considering the music from the point of view of its style, the sum of all its "personality" traits. The early twelfth- and thirteenth-century songs represent monophony, the purest melody unencumbered by harmony. Until the ninth and tenth centuries this had been the normal manner of music all over the world. When the author of *Sir Orfeo* (c. 1300) pictured the dinner music provided by " . . . trompours and tabourers, Harpours fele, and crouders. Miche melody thay maked all . . . " he stressed this element of melody, the foundation for such great treasuries of medieval music as Gregorian chant, the songs of the Provençal *trobador* and the French *trouvère*, the Spanish *Cantigas*, and the Italian *Laude*.

Though the annals of early polyphony (the new art of combined melody) ring with names like Chartres, St. Martial in Limoges, and Paris, England was soon to take a hand in the game, and according to her own rules at that. During the years of French Gothic hegemony, music was dominated by the "perfect" intervals, the octave, fifth, and fourth, producing austere and hollow (though by no means unpleasant) sounds. Theory ruled these intervals perfect, and practice followed theory, since medieval man customarily trusted any authority save his own senses. The English, however, seemed to prefer the more suave third and sixth, in spite of the fact that theoretical tomes decreed these intervals "imperfect." Our seven pieces of early polyphony (Nos. 5–11), are very different one from another but share in common a characteristic English love of full sound and of harmony based on the third: the melodious duo, *Edi Beo;* the beloved, bouncing Sumer canon, an outstanding musical achievement, though scholars argue over its date of birth; the Worcester *Alleluya Psallat,* surely the most cheerful *Alleluia* on record and one of the most grateful medieval compositions; the sacred pieces by Power and Roy Henry from the *Old Hall* manuscript.

Early fifteenth-century music, whose sweetly "pan-consonant" sound was now established in both English and continental styles, is illustrated here by a motet of the first English composer, John Dunstable and by some lively carols, one of which celebrates Henry V's victory at Agincourt in 1415.

Secular music burgeoned from the musically fertile sixteenth century, a good deal of it issuing from courtly centers where music and letters were cultivated. Such a group of poets and musicians surrounded Henry VIII. We find an index of their activities in a beautifully written manuscript which is the source for Nos. 17–20, part songs by the King himself and by William Cornysh. Modeled on French courtly *chansons,* these songs are polyphonic, though simply so. A radically different style distinguishes the church music of Henry's generation. In the works of masters like Taverner and Tallis, the traditional penchant for full sonority and for mildly acid chromatic clashings, especially at cadences, is joined to elements from Flemish Renaissance style — high-arching and winding melodic lines and complicated part weaving. Tallis and Byrd sum up this synthesis in England's last great Catholic music.

If Queen Elizabeth's time witnessed the disastrous failure of the Spanish Armada, it also saw a decisive victory of High Renaissance Italian culture over England. In music, forms like the madrigal and its lighter brethren, the *canzonetta* and *balletto,* were welcomed, translated, and ultimately transformed. Byrd, who wrote the first English madrigals "after the Italian vaine," betrays some uneasy national pride by rejecting the Italianate term, preferring to call his madrigalian publications *Songes.* Morley, on the other hand, accepted the Italian bounty wholeheartedly. After a study of his models, in the course of which he published two books of Italian madrigals with translated texts, he effected a fusion of both serious and light foreign types with native English spirit. The resulting English madrigal was no mean achievement. Its vitality and freshness is especially striking when we consider that its model, which had begun life some fifty years earlier, was now rather overripe and tired. The Italian composers most favored were Croce and Marenzio. Gesualdo's supercharged manneristic experiments were also appreciated, some of his harmonic findings being used to good effect by Dowland, Wilbye, and Weelkes, the serious madrigalists. Morley, though so eminently associated with the light touch, could also turn out as grave and poignant a madrigal as the rest (see Nos. 28 and 29).

A specifically English contribution to the madrigal family was the ayre. This could be performed in two ways — as a part song (Nos. 31–32) or as a solo song to the lute (see *An Elizabethan Song Book* for a collection of lute ayres). Many of the madrigalists published volumes of ayres, although the genre seems to have encouraged composers like John Dowland, the poet-musician Thomas Campion, and Robert Jones to devote themselves almost exclusively to it.

After Elizabeth's death in 1603, moods of pessimism and doubt presaged in art works produced during her reign emerged so clearly that scholars speak of the "Jacobean melancholy." This new intensity of feeling blended very well with a similar trend imported from Italy — the "New Music" developed in Florence and Mantua. Here the emphasis was placed on solo song, performed so as to wring the utmost in affective expression from intense and sensual verse. The impact of the new style was not immediately felt in the sphere of the polyphonic song, but rather in masque music and the ayres by such composers as Alfonso Ferrabosco, Jr., John Coprario, John Daniel, and Dowland. At least one master, Tomkins, ignored these trends entirely, and continued to compose in the vein of Byrd, his teacher, well into the Caroline age.

Once there was a brand of Victorian madness which claimed that Englishmen were unmusical. A glance at this volume should kill off any lingering symptoms of that disease; for England was once a true nest of singing birds. Eminent foreigners sounded the praises of her musical achievements unhesitatingly. But certain modern apologists have overstated the case in the propagandistic spirit of the opening of Morley's theoretical book, *Plaine and Easie Introduction to Practicall Musicke* where hapless Philomathes tells of his shame when, after being requested to sing madrigals with the other guests after dinner, he had to admit that he could not and, in his words, "every one began to wonder; yea, some whispered to others demanding how I was brought up, so that upon shame of mine ignorance I go now to seek out mine old friend Master Gnorimus [Morley himself], to make myself his scholar." Nowadays we interpret such documents with caution. We do not believe that every Elizabethan courtier could read off a madrigal part at sight. But we do believe that a substantial number of intelligentsia in the Renaissance could function musically. And those others, unlike today's crop of passive music lovers, knew at least that they ought to be able to take part, because their courtiers' handbooks told them so! The Tudors alone furnish an exemplary instance. Is there a ruler alive today who could live up to a Venetian ambassador's description of Henry VIII as ". . . very accomplished; a good musician; composes well; is a most capital horseman; a fine jouster; speakes good French, Latin and Spanish . . ."? Another Venetian envoy reported that Queen Mary "takes great pleasure in playing on the lute and spinet, and is a very good performer on both instruments; and indeed before her accession she taught many of her maids of honour . . . " There seems no need to cite any of the documents vouching for Elizabeth's proficiency.

In short, a very healthy amateur tradition obtained. It was by no means limited to royalty, although compositions by a Lancaster and a Tudor take well-merited places in these pages. The most interesting thing is that this tradition coexisted with the other tradition of mastery and virtuosity. The master's nimbleness did not at that time disenchant the bumbling amateur, though a regrettable schism was to grow increasingly pronounced, beginning in the baroque age. In our own time it is the amateur who furnishes the enthusiastic audience for music from before 1750; the professional musician, trained in the spirit of the romantic movement, tends to look at it askance. But "Time and love with gladnesse, Once ere long will provide for this . . . " as Morley sang, and will heal the estrangement. In the process, which goes on apace, collections such as this one, lovingly compiled by a skilled musician associated with highly professional performance standards, can provide balm.

Columbia University   Joel Newman

SOME SUGGESTED READING

Auden, W. H. "Words and Notes." Introduction to *An Elizabethan Song Book* (Doubleday, New York, 1955)

Bukofzer, Manfred. *Studies in Medieval & Renaissance Music* (Norton, New York, 1950)

   "Sumer Is Icumen In," A Revision (U. of Calif., Berkeley, 1944)

Greene, Richard L. *The Early English Carols* (Oxford, 1935). Introduction

Grove's Dictionary of Music and Musicians, 5th edition (St. Martin's Press, New York, 1955). Biographical articles

Harrison, Frank L. *Music in Medieval Britain* (Routledge, London, 1958)

Mellers, Wilfrid. "Words and Music in Elizabethan England," in *The Age of Shakespeare,* ed. by Boris Ford (Penguin, London, 1956). Pp. 386–415

New Oxford History of Music
   Vol. II: Early Medieval Music up to 1300 (Oxford, London, 1954)
   Vol. III: Ars Nova and the Renaissance (Oxford, London, 1959)

Reese, Gustave. *Music in the Middle Ages* (Norton, New York, 1940). Chapter 14
   Music in the Renaissance (Norton, New York, 1954). Chapter 15

Woodfill, Walter L. *Musicians in English Society from Elizabeth to Charles I* (Princeton, 1953)

NOTE ON EDITORIAL POLICY

The following rules were observed by the editor in preparing this volume:

Bar lines have been added throughout, there being none in the original. These have been placed at regular metrical intervals where possible.

Dynamics and tempo indications are editorial and are intended merely as suggestions to the performer.

Note values have in most cases been reduced to one half or one quarter of the original values.

Accidentals indicated in parentheses are editorial; those appearing without parentheses before the notes are original; accidentals above the note, without parentheses, are warning signs.

Text underlay and spelling is original wherever possible and editorial underlay appears in italics.

Time signatures in brackets are editorial.

Although the pieces have been transcribed in their original keys, the performers should have no hesitation about transposing to higher or lower keys to suit the requirements of their vocal ensemble.

CRIST AND SAINTE MARIE

ST. GODRIC (*died* 1170)

Monophonic song forms an important part of the music of the Middle
Ages, and its roots lie in the great plainsong literature of early times.
Following the Norman Conquest, the earliest surviving English songs are
those of St. Godric, a Saxon who lived a hermit's existence in Northern
England during the twelfth century. His *Crist and Sainte Marie* can
best be described as a miniature drama in which Godric's dead sister,
surrounded by angels, tells of her journey to heaven.

e   Swa   on   sca-   mel   me   i-

led- - -   de   that   ic   on   this-   *se*

er- -   de   ne   sil- - -   de   Wid

mi-   ne   ba-   re   fo-   te   i-   tre- di- -   e.

1st tempo
Angels again:

Ky-   ri- e- ley-   son.   Chri- ste-   ley-   son.

Angels again:

Ky-   ri- e- ley- son.   Chri- ste   e-   le-   y-   son.

CRIST AND SAINTE MARIE

> Lord have mercy.
> Christ have mercy.
> Christ and St. Mary so led me on a footstool
> that I did not tread on this earth with my bare foot.
> Lord have mercy. Christ have mercy.
> Lord have mercy. Christ have mercy.

MAN MEI LONGE

ANONYMOUS (XIIIth *century*)

MAN MEI LONGE

The art of the troubadour and trouvère—along with its Spanish and German counterparts—survives in many continental manuscripts. Though English minstrel songs were widely sung throughout medieval Britain by the wandering poet-musicians, very little of this music remains. *Man mei longe* and *Worldes blis ne last* are two moralizing songs whose melancholy mood is in sharp contrast to the spirited English instrumental dance music of this period.

re- - - ne, an fer- li- che ____ ma-
ket is blench. Thar- vo- re, man, thu
the bi- thench, ____ al sel va- lu-
i the gre- ne, wel- a- wey! nis
King ne Que- ne that ne sel
drin- ke of deth- is drench. Man, er thu
fal- le of thi_ bench, thu sin- ne a- quench.

MAN MEI LONGE

Long may man ween his life to be but oft for him there waits a trick;
fair weather often turns to rain, and sunshine is wondrously made.
Therefore, man, bethink thyself—all thy green youth shall fade. Well-
a-day! there is neither king nor queen who shall not drink the draught
of death. Man, ere thou fallest off thy bench, quench thy sin.

WORLDES BLIS NE LAST

ANONYMOUS (XIIIth century)

World-es_____ blis ne last no_____

thro- we, Hit wit ant wend a- wey a-

non.____ The leng- ur that hich____ hit i-

kno- we,__ The lasse hic____ find- e_____

pris ther- on. __ For al hit __ is i-

meynd wyd __ ka- re, Mid so- re- we ant wid __

u- vel __ fa- re, Ant at the last- e

poue- re ant ba- re Hit let mon wen hit

gin- net a- gon. Al the blis- se, this __

he- re ant __ the- re __ Bi- lou- keth at __

hend- e __ wop ant __ mon. __

WORLDES BLIS NE LAST

The world's joy lasts no time at all, it departs and fades away at once.
The longer I know it, the less value I find in it. For it is all mixed
with troubles, with sorrows and misfortune, and at the last, when it begins
to pass away, it leaves a man poor and naked. All the joy, both here
and there, is finally encompassed by weeping and lamentation.

JESU CRISTES MILDE MODER

ANONYMOUS (XIIIth century)

The anonymous pieces *Jesu Cristes milde moder* and *Edi beo thu hevene Quene* are beautiful examples of early polyphony. They are composed in the *gymel* style—a kind of English duo writing that favors the intervals "third" and "sixth" and creates the illusion of two voices moving in parallel motion when, in actuality, they always cross each other. Both pieces date from the second half of the thirteenth century. Because of their length only the opening and closing verses of *Jesu. Cristes* and the first stanza of *Edi beo* are given.

that he was i- pi- ned on.

pp The sone heng, the mo- der stud ⎯⎯

and bi- held hire child- es blud ⎯⎯

wu it of hise wund- es ran.

stronger
mf Neu- e blis- se he us brou- te

that man- kin so de- re bou- te,

and for us gaf is de- re lif.

f Glade and bli- the thu us ma- ke

for thi swe- te so- nes sa- ke,

e- di mai- den blis- ful wif.

Quen of e- vene for thi blis- se

lithe al hu- re so- ri- nes- se

31

JESU CRISTES MILDE MODER

Jesu Cristes gentle mother stood and beheld her son pinned to the cross. The son hung, the mother stood and beheld her child's blood running from his wounds. New bliss he brought, bought dearly for mankind, and he gave his dear life for us. Thou makest us glad and blithe for thy sweet son's sake, be thou blissful, virgin wife!

EDI BEO THU HEVENE QUENE

ANONYMOUS (XIV*th century*)

Joyful and fast

T&B (S&A) *mf* E- di be- o thu hev- en- e

T&B (S&A) *mf*

quen- e fol- kes frou- re and eng- les

(*p*)

blis. Mo- der un- wem- med and maid- en

cle- ne swich____ in world non

EDI BEO THU HEVENE QUENE

Happy be thou, heavenly Queen, man's comfort and angel's bliss.
Mother unstained and maiden clean, such in world none other is.
Of thee easily it is seen that of all women thou hast the prize.
My sweet lady, hear my boon and rue of me if thy will is.

SUMER IS ICUMEN IN

ANONYMOUS (XIV*th century*)

This is the most famous of all medieval compositions and appears here
in the version by the late Manfred Bukofzer. There has been dispute
among scholars about this remarkable canonic piece. It is traditionally
dated from the thirteenth century, but Bukofzer has attempted to prove
that it is from the early fourteenth. His transcription restores what
appears to be the duple meter and *Cu-cu* call (see measure 19, highest
part) of the original, apparently altered by a later scribe.

37

38

39

40

41

ALLELUYA PSALLAT

ANONYMOUS (*early* XIV*th century*)

This glorious *Alleluya* comes to us from a body of sacred music known to scholars as the Worcester Fragments, remnants of a great repertoire composed in the late thirteenth and early fourteenth centuries for Worcester Cathedral. Although the music shows the influence of an earlier French tradition, employing techniques more conservative than those used in the contemporary French style, one sees here the emergence of a rich English polyphonic art.

44

ALLELUYA PSALLAT

Alleluia sings this congregation, Alleluia, with cymbals and zithers, Alleluia, the joyous crowd in harmony sings, Alleluia, to God praise and glory. Alleluia.

ANGELUS AD VIRGINEM

ANONYMOUS (XIVth century)

Chaucer, describing Nicholas, the clerk, in the "Miller's Tale," writes:

> And all above ther lay a gay sautrye,
> On which he made a-nightes melodye,
> So swetely that al the chamber rang,
> And Angelus ad Virginem he sang.

This tune and polyphonic settings of it appear in the thirteenth century, and Chaucer's reference one hundred years later attests to its great popularity. In this version the melody lies in the middle voice, and the harmony is based on a progression of triads of the first inversion—a style distinctly English in origin.

ve; vir- gi- nis for- mi- di-

ve; vir- gi- nis for- mi- di-

ve; vir- gi- nis for- mi- di-

nem de- mul- cens in- quit, A-

nem de- mul- cens in- quit, A-

nem de- mul- cens in- quit, A-

ve! *f* A- ve, re- gi na

ve! *f* A- ve, re- gi na

ve! *f* A- ve, re- gi na

vir- gi- num! *mf* ce- li ter-

vir- gi- num! *mf* ce- li ter-

vir- gi- num! *mf* ce- li ter-

re que Do- mi- num con-

re que Do- mi- num con-

re que Do- mi- num con-

47

ANGELUS AD VIRGINEM

The Angel said to the Virgin, stealing into the chamber and calming her fearfulness: Hail, Queen of Virgins, the Lord of heaven and earth shalt thou conceive and bear in virginity, the saviour of man; thou art become the gate of heaven and redressor of wrongs.

J.N.

BEATA PROGENIES

LEONEL POWER (*died* 1445)

Leonel Power was one of the great masters of the first half of the fifteenth century, but very little is known of his life other than his possible connection with Christ Church, Canterbury. As with his more famous contemporary, Dunstable, Leonel reflects the rich cultural interchange between England and France during this period. The delicate *Beata progenies*, which appears in the Old Hall Manuscript, is written in a simple style, employing a plainsong melody in the middle voice.

49

un- — — de Chri- stus — na-
un- — — de Chri- stus — na-
un- — — — de Chri- stus — na-

tus — — est; *mf* Quam glo-
tus — est; *mf* Quam glo-
tus — — est; *mf* Quam glo-

ri- o- — — — sa —
ri- o- — — — sa —
ri- — o- — — — sa —

— est — Vir- — — — go
— est — Vir- — — go
— est — Vir- — — — go

BEATA PROGENIES

Blessed progeny whence Christ was born. How glorious is the Virgin who gave birth to the King of heaven!

ALAS DEPARTYNGE IS
GROUND OF WOO

ANONYMOUS (XV*th century*)

A considerable quantity of medieval English sacred music has survived, but pitifully few examples of secular song remain. The anonymous *Alas departynge is ground of woo*—one of a number of songs with English text found in continental sources—appears in the Mellon *Chansonnier*, a collection of Burgundian origin now at Yale University. In the original the upper part is without text; it has been added here so that the piece may be performed by two singers.

53

SANCTA MARIA

JOHN DUNSTABLE (*c.* 1370-1453)

One of the greatest composers of his time, Dunstable was musician to the Duke of Bedford during the reigns of Henry V and VI. His music was well known on the continent and exerted a strong influence on the young Burgundian musicians, Dufay and Binchois. The bulk of his compositions survive in continental manuscripts rather than English ones, perhaps because of his travels in Europe. The Marian motet *Sancta Maria* can be performed either as an alto solo with two instruments or for voices alone.

55

56

SANCTA MARIA

Holy Mary, in this world there has arisen none like you among women.
Blooming like the rose, fragrant as the lily, pray for us, holy Mother
of God.

SANCTUS

ROY HENRY (HENRY IV [?] 1367-1413)

One of the most important sources of medieval polyphony is the Old Hall manuscript, a large collection of sacred works by English and continental composers. Two of the compositions are by a *Roy Henry*, and recent evidence seems to indicate this was Henry IV. His travels in Europe, before he ascended the throne in 1399, acquainted him with the magnificent households of Charles VI of France, the Duke of Berry, and Philip the Bold. The rich musical life of the Royal Chapels of the Lancastrian kings was indebted to such continental models.

59

SANCTUS

Holy, Holy, Holy, Lord of hosts. Heaven and earth are full of Thy glory. Hosanna in the highest! Blessed is he that cometh in the name of the Lord. Hosanna in the highest!

DEO GRACIAS ANGLIA

The Agincourt Carol

ANONYMOUS (XV*th century*)

Over one hundred carols with music are preserved in English fifteenth-century manuscripts. These exciting pieces were written for every occasion, not only Christmas. Their dancelike rhythms, repetitive form, catchy tunes (which usually lie in the lowest part), and mixed Latin and English texts indicate they were designed for popular use rather than for the court. The "Verse" portions sound best when sung by solo voices. The refrain sections, marked "Chorus" in the original, precede and follow each verse, distinguishing the carol from other English forms.

VERSE

1. Owre kynge went forth to Nor-man-dy With grace and myght of chy-val-ry; Ther God for hym wrought merve-lus-ly; Wher-fore Eng-londe may calle and cry, 'De-o gra-ci-as.

1. Owre kynge went forth to Nor-man-dy With grace and myght of chy-val-ry; Ther God for hym wrought merve-lus-ly; Wher-fore Eng-londe may calle and cry, 'De-o gra-ci-as.'

attacca

63

Chorus B is sung after each verse.

2.

He sette a sege, the sothe for
 to say,
To Harflu toune with ryal aray;
That toune he wan and made a
 fray
That Fraunce shal rywe tyl
 domesday;
 Deo gracias.

3.

Than went oure kynge with alle his
 oste
Throwe Fraunce, for alle the Freshe
 boste;
He spared no drede of lest ne
 moste
Tyl he come to Agincourt coste;
 Deo gracias.

4.

Than, forsoth, that knyght comely,
In Agincourt feld he faught manly;
Thorw grace of God most myghty
He had bothe the felde and the
    victory;
    Deo gracias.

5.

There dukys and erlys, lorde and
    barone
Were take and slayne, and that wel
    sone,
And summe were ladde into
    Lundone
With joye and merthe and grete
    renone;
    Deo gracias.

6.

Now gracious God he save oure
    kynge,
His peple, and alle his wel-wyllynge;
Yef hym gode lyfe and gode
    endynge,
That we with merth mowe savely
    synge;
    Deo gracias.

DEO GRACIAS ANGLIA
  The Agincourt Carol

Deo gracias Anglia/Redde pro victoria—Render thanks to God, England,
for victory; *Yef*—grant.

NOVA, NOVA

ANONYMOUS (xvth century)

2.

He mete a maydyn in a place;
He kneled down before her face;
He sayd, 'Hayle, Mary, full of
  grace.'
Nova, nova.

3.

When the maydyn sawe all this,
She was sore abashed, ywys,
Lest that she had done amys;
Nova, nova.

4.

Then sayd the angell, 'Dred not
  you:
Ye shall conceyve in all vertu
A chyld whose name shall be
  Jhesu.'
Nova, nova.

5.

Then sayd the mayd, 'How may
  this be,
Godes son to be born of me?
I know not of manys carnalite.'
Nova, nova.

6.

Then said the angell anon ryght,
'The Holy Gost ys on the plyght;
Ther ys nothyng unpossible to God
  Almyght.'
Nova, nova.

7.

Then sayd the angell anon,
'Ytt ys not fully vi moneth agon
Syth Seynt Elizabeth conceyved
  Seynt Johan.'
Nova, nova.

8.

Then sayd the mayd anon a-hye,
'I am Godes own truly;
  Ecce ancilla Domini.'
  Nova, nova.

Chorus is sung after each verse.

NOVA, NOVA

Nova, nova 'Ave' fitt ex 'Eva'—News, news, "Hail" is made from "Eve"
(Eve's original sin is transformed into Gabriel's salutation). *Ecce ancilla Domini*—Behold the Lord's handmaiden.

NOWEL SYNG WE BOTHE
AL AND SOM

ANONYMOUS (XVth century)

Boisterously and fast

No- wel syng we ___ bothe al ___ and

No- wel syng we bothe al and

som, Now Rex Pa- ci- fi- cus ys ___ y- come.

som, Now Rex Pa- ci- fi- cus ys y- come.

VERSE

Ex- or- tum est ___ in love ___ and lysse: Now

Ex- or- tum est in love and lysse: Now

69

2.

De fructu ventris of Mary bryght:
Bothe God and man in here alyght;
Owte of dysese he dyde us dyght,
    Bothe alle and summe.

3.

Puer natus to us was sent,
To blysse us bought, fro bale us
    blent,
And ellys to wo we hadde ywent,
    Bothe alle and summe.

4.

Lux fulgebit with love and lyght,
In Mary mylde his pynon pyght,
In here toke kynde with manly
    myght,
    Bothe alle and summe.

5.

Gloria tibi ay and blysse:
God unto his grace he us wysse,
The rent of heven that we not
    mysse,
    Bothe alle and summe.

Chorus is sung after each verse.

NOWEL SYNG WE BOTHE AL AND SOM

Rex Pacificus—King of Peace. *Exortum est*—He is born. *De fructu ventris*
—of the fruit of thy womb. *Puer natus*—A Son is born. *Lux fulgebit*—a
light will shine. *Gloria tibi*—Glory to Thee.

lysse—joy; *gysse*—prepare; *dyght*—put; *blent*—took; *his pennon pyght*—set
up his pennant; *wysse*—guide; *rent*—reward.

QUID PETIS O FILI

RICHARD PYGOTT (*c.* 1485-*c.* 1552)

Pygott was master of the choir in Cardinal Wolsey's private chapel and, later, a member of Henry VIIIth's Royal Household Chapel. His lovely carol *Quid petis o fili* appears in a manuscript collection dating from the early 1500's (British Museum Additional Manuscript 31922), which contains vocal and instrumental music written for the court of Henry VIII. Although this piece still uses the verse-refrain form and the macaronic English and Latin text of the medieval carol, its continuous imitative technique marks it as a work of the Renaissance.

mi- hi plau-sus os- cu- la ____ da ____ da.

os- cu- la ____ da ____ da.

____ da ____ da.

da da.

VERSE I*
somewhat marked

S

A

T
mf The mo- der full man- er- ly and mek-

B
mf The mo- der full man- er- ly and mek-

*the verses are best sung by solo voices.

mf lok-yng on her lyt- till son, so laugh-yng in

ly as a mayd lok- yng on her lyt- till son, so laugh-

ly as a mayd

74

REPEAT REFRAIN FROM SIGN

VERSE II
a bit slower

I mene this by Ma-ry, oure mak-er's
mo-der of myght, full love-ly look-yng on our Lord, the
lan-terne of lyght, thus sa-yng to our sa-vi-our, this saw I
in my syght, this re-son that I rede you now, I rede it full
ryght.

REFRAIN
Quid

77

with motion

S — *mf* Mus- yng on her

T — *mf* Mus- yng on her man- ers so

B — *mf* Mus-yng on her man- ers so my mard

man- ers so my mard was my mayne, save it

my mard was _____ my mayne, _____ save _____

was my mayne, save it

ples- yd me so pass- yng- ly that past was my

_____ it ples- yd me so pass- yng- ly that _____

ples- yd me so pass- yng- ly that past was my

payn, (-ayn) _____

_____ pass- yd was my payn, _____ *p* yet

payn, _____ *p* yet soft- ly

QUID PETIS O FILI

What do you wish, O sweetest
Mother of the Son, ba, ba, ba, ba?
O Father, O Son,
Give me fond kisses, da, da, da, da.

WITH OWT DYSCORDE

KING HENRY VIII (1491-1547)

"For the Kynge hime self beinge miche delited to synge, and Sir Peter Carewe havinge a pleasaunte voyce, the Kynge woulde very often use hyme to synge with hime certeyne songes they called *fremen* songs, as namely, 'By the banke as I lay,' and 'As I walked the wode so wylde,' &c." So writes a chronicler of Henry's music-making which, from all the evidence, was extensive. His instrumental collection was very large, the finest European and English musicians were in his employ, and he composed some rather good *chansons* and instrumental pieces. The two pieces printed here, are in French style and appear in British Museum Add. Ms. 31922.

WITH OWT DYSCORDE

Wher for now we
that lovers be

let us now pray.

Onys love sure
ffor to procure

with owt denay.

Wher love so sewith
ther no hart rewith

but condyscend.

Yf contrarye
What remedy

god yt amend.

O MY HART

KING HENRY VIII

A ROBYN, GENTIL ROBYN

WILLIAM CORNYSH (*died c.* 1523)

William Cornysh was composer and poet at the court of Henry VIII. From 1509 to 1523 he held the post of Master of the Children at the Chapel Royal which entailed conducting the choir, composing music for the services, preparing musical activities, and staging entertainments for the court. *A Robyn* is the setting of a poem by Sir Thomas Wyatt, referred to almost a century later in Shakespeare's *Twelfth Night* (Act IV, sc. 2). Both Cornysh pieces are from the British Museum Ms. already cited.

myne. *p* A Rob- yn, gen- til Rob- yn,

p

tel me how thy le- man doth and thow shalt know of

myne. *mf* A Rob- yn, gen- til Rob- yn,

mf

mf A Rob- yn, gen- til Rob- yn,

tel me how thy le- mandoth and thow shalt know of

tel me how thy le- man doth and thow shalt know of

myne. *p* A Rob- yn, gen- til Rob-

myne. *p*

myne. *mf* My la- dy is un- kynde I wis, a- lac why is she

yn, tel me how thy le- man doth and thow shalt know of

so, she lov'th an- oth- er bet- ter than me and yet she will say

myne. *mf* A Rob- yn, gen- til Rob- yn,

no. *mf* A Rob- yn, gen- til Rob- yn,

tel me how thy le- man doth and thow shalt know of myne.

tel me how thy le- man doth and thow shalt know of myne. *mf* I

86

BLOW THY HORNE HUNTER

WILLIAM CORNYSH

BLOW THY HORNE, HUNTER

Sore thus dere strykyn ys and yet she bled no whytt,
she lay so fayre, I cowde nott mys, lord I was glad of it.
    REFRAIN *Now blow thy horne hunter*
                and blow thy horne joly hunter.

As I stod under a banke the dere shoffe on the mede,
I stroke her so that downe she sanke, but yet she was not dede.
           Now blow thy horne &c.

Ther she gothe, se ye nott, how she gothe over the playne,
And yf ye lust to have a shott, I warrant her barrayne.
           Now blow thy horne &c.

He to go and I to go but he ran fast a fore,
I had hym shott and strik the do for I myght shott no more.
           Now blow thy horne &c.

To the covert bothe thay went, for I fownd wher she lay,
An arrow in her hanch she hent, for faynte she myght nott bray.
           Now blow thy horne &c.

I was wery of the game, I went to tavern to drynk,
now the construcyon on the same, what do yow meane or thynk.
           Now blow thy horne &c.

Here I leve and mak an end now of this hunters lore,
I thynk his bow ys well unbent, hys bolt may fle no more.
           Now blow thy horne &c.

GLORIA

JOHN TAVERNER (*c.* 1495-1545)

Taverner's liturgical works are a monumental contribution to early sixteenth-century English music. The *Western Wynde* Mass, from which this *Gloria* is taken, is based on the song of that name. This is a splendid example of Taverner's art: the ornate counterpoint enmeshes the ever-present melody in a polyphonic web without, however, obscuring the song-like quality of the composition. The words *Gloria in excelsis Deo* are not set, since it was Renaissance practice to have the priest intone them.

f Do- mi- ne _____ de- us, rex

f Do- mi- ne de- us, rex coe- le- -

f Do- mi- ne de- us, rex coe- le- stis,

f Do- mi- ne _____ de- us, rex coe- le- -

coe- le- stis, de- us pa- - ter _____ o-mni-po-

stis, de- us pa- - ter o- mni- - po-

de- us pa- - - ter o- mni- -

- - stis, de- us pa- - ter o-

tens. Do-mi- ne fi- - -

- - - - - - tens. Do- mi- ne _____ fi-

po- - - - tens. Do-mi- ne _____ fi- -

mni- - po- - - tens. Do- mi- ne _____

GLORIA

(Glory to God in the highest) And on earth peace to men of good will. We praise Thee. We bless Thee. We adore Thee. We glorify Thee. We give thanks to Thee for Thy great glory. O Lord God, heavenly king, God the Father almighty. O Lord, the only-begotten son, Jesus Christ. Lord God, Lamb of God, Son of the Father.

EDITOR'S NOTE: The following verse is the secular text to the melody as it appears in Brit. Mus. Ms. App. 58:

> Westron wynde when wyll thow blow
> the small rayne down can rayne
> Cryst yf my love wer in my armys
> And I yn my bed Agayne.

AGNUS DEI

THOMAS TALLIS (*c.* 1505-1585)

"He serv'd long Tyme in Chappell with grete prayse,
Fower Sovereygnes Reygnes (a thing not often seen)
I mean Kyng Henry and Prince Edward's Dayes,
Quene Mary and Elizabeth our Quene."

from Tallis' epitaph

Tallis' works represent the full flowering of Renaissance music in England. His greatest compositions were those written for the Latin Service —works charged with deep emotion and executed with the greatest craftsmanship. This music, while influenced by the continental masters, is unmistakably in the English tradition. The *Agnus Dei* is from his Mass for four voices, probably an early work; the *Salvator mundi* is from *Cantiones sacrae,* a collection of motets by Tallis and Byrd, printed in 1575.

102

AGNUS DEI

Lamb of God, who takest away the sins of the world, have mercy on us.
Lamb of God, who takest away the sins of the world, have mercy on us.
Lamb of God, who takest away the sins of the world, grant us peace.

SALVATOR MUNDI

THOMAS TALLIS

105

SALVATOR MUNDI

Saviour of the world, save us. Thou who hast redeemed us by the Cross
and thy blood, help us, we pray thee, our God.

J.N.

SUSANNA FAYRE
SOMETIME ASSAULTED WAS

WILLIAM BYRD (1543-1623)

The most esteemed and prolific English composer of his time, William Byrd represents the late Renaissance style at its very best. He wrote in all the forms and for all the media known to the sixteenth century: madrigals; solo songs; music for viol ensemble; solo instrumental pieces for organ, lute, and harpsichord; anthems and Services for the English Church; Latin masses and motets. The great variety of his output is equaled by few musicians of any period. The Penitential motet, *Emendemus in melius,* is from *Cantiones sacrae* (1575). The settings of the "Susanna and the Elders" story and the description of Dido's death are from *Songs of Sundrie Natures* (1589).

110

ti- tie shall then de-flour- ed bee, which is. so deere to

then de- flour- ed bee, de- flour-ed bee, which is so deere to

shall then de- flour-ed bee, which is so deere to mee, to

mee, that I de- test my lyfe,

mee, to mee, that I de- test my

mee, that I de- test my lyfe, my

my lyfe, if it ____ be- reft- ed be from me,

lyfe, my lyfe, ___ if it be- reft- ed be from

lyfe, if it be- reft- ed be from me, ___

____ from me, *f* and rath- er would I dye

me, from me, *f* and rath- er

f and rath- er would I dye ____ of mine ___

113

114

EMENDEMUS IN MELIUS

WILLIAM BYRD

116

119

EMENDEMUS IN MELIUS

Let us make amends for sinning in ignorance; lest suddenly overtaken
by the day of death, we seek space for penance, and are not able to
find it. Attend, O Lord, and have mercy, for we have sinned against
Thee. Help us, O God, our Saviour: and for the honor of Thy name,
O Lord, deliver us.

J.N.

WHEN FIRST BY FORCE
OF FATALL DESTENIE

WILLIAM BYRD

ABOUT THE MAY POLE

THOMAS MORLEY (1557-1603?)

The Italian vogue that overtook England during Elizabeth's rule brought with it the musical fashions current in Venice and Rome. As editor, Morley popularized the madrigal, publishing collections of music by Italy's leading composers. His own madrigals, ballets, and canzonets are patterned after Italian forms, but have a distinctly Elizabethan flavor that distinguishes them from their models. The pieces here are from Morley's *First Booke of Balletts* (1595), *Canzonets...to three voyces* (1593), and *Canzonets to two voyces* (1595).

128

la la la la la. Fa la la la la la la la. A- la. And

Fa la la la la la la la la. A- la. And

la. Fa la la la la la la la. A- la. And

la la la. Fa la la la la. A- la. And

la. Fa la la la la la. A- la. And

to the wan-ton In- stru-ment still they went toe and

to the wan-ton In- stru-ment still they went toe and

to the wan-ton In- stru-ment still they went toe and

to the wan-ton In- stru-ment still they went toe and

to the wan-ton In- stru-ment

ABOUT THE MAY POLE

VERSE II

The Sheperds and the Nimphes them round enclosed had,
Wondring with what facilitie,
About they turnd them in such strange agilitie. Fa la la.
And still when they unlosed had,
With words full of delight they gently kissed them,
And thus sweetly to sing they never missed them.

LEAVE ALAS THIS TORMENTING

THOMAS MORLEY

134

135

skill not, For thus I will not, for
skill not, For thus I will not,
it skill not, For thus I will not, for
skill not, For thus I will not, for thus I will
skill not, For thus I will not, for

thus I will not, Now con-tent- ed, Then tor-
Now con-tent- ed, Then tor-
thus I will not, Now con-tent- ed, Then tor-
not, I will ____ not, Now con- tent- ed, Then tor-
thus I will not, Now con- tent- ed, Then tor-

somewhat slower

1st tempo

guish,   *p* live _____ in   love   and   lan -

_____ in   love   and   lan- guish,   live _____ in

guish,   *p* live_____ in   love   and   lan -

p live_____ in   love   and   lan -   guish, live in

p live _____ in   love   and

1st   **2nd**

- - - - guish.   -guish.

love   and   lan- guish.   -guish.

guish, and   lan- guish.   *mf* For   -guish.

love   and   lan- guish. *mf* For thus I will   -guish.

lan- - - guish.   *mf* For thus I   -guish.

CEASE MINE EYES

THOMAS MORLEY

your la- ment- ing, O cease, a- las, O cease, a- las, this your la-

ing, cease, O a- las, O cease, a- las, this your

eyes, cease your la- ment- ing, your la- ment-

ment- - ing: in vaine, in vaine, in vaine you hope, you

la- ment- ing: in vaine, in vaine it is

ing: in vaine, in vaine, in vaine you hope,

hope in vaine of hir hard harts re- lent- - -

to hope of hir hard harts re- lent- - - -

you hope of hir hard harts re-

140

141

I GOE BEFORE MY DARLING

THOMAS MORLEY

ling, I goe be- fore my dar - - -

fore my dar - - - - ling, I goe be-

- - ling, I goe be- fore my dar -

fore my dar - - ling, I goe be- fore my dar-

- - - ling. *p* Fol-low thou to the bowre in the close

- - - ling, *p* Fol- low thou to the bowre in the close

precisely

al - - ley, Ther wee will to- geth-

al - ley, Ther wee will to- geth- er,

146

er, Sweet-ly kisse each eyth- er, And like two wan-tons,

Sweet-ly kisse each eyth- er, And like two wan-tons,

f Dal- ly dal- ly dal- ly dal- ly dal- ly dal- ly dal-

f Dal- ly dal- ly dal- ly dal- ly dal-

ly dal- ly dal- ly dal- ly dal- ly dal- ly

ly dal- ly dal- ly dal- ly dal- ly dal- ly

dal- ly dal- ly dal- ly. *p* There wee will to-

dal- ly dal- ly dal- ly. *p* There wee

geth- er, Sweet- ly kisse each eyth- er, And

will to- geth- er, Sweet- ly kisse each eyth- er, And

lyke two wan- tons,

lyke two wan- tons, *f* Dal- ly dal- ly

f Dal- ly dal- ly dal- ly dal- ly dal- ly dal- ly

dal- ly dal- ly dal- ly dal- ly dal- ly

dal- ly dal- ly dal- ly dal- ly dal- ly dal- ly dal- ly.

dal- ly dal- ly dal- ly dal- ly dal- ly dal- ly dal- ly.

TOSSE NOT MY SOULE

JOHN DOWLAND (1563-1626)

Dowland was the most famous lutenist-composer of his time. His instrumental music and airs were known in England and on the continent, since he traveled widely and performed in Italy, Germany, France, Denmark, and the Low Countries. Dowland's magnificent songs, his virtuoso fantasies for lute, and superb dances for instrumental ensemble have no peers in late sixteenth and early seventeenth-century music. Included here are two songs from his second (1600) and third (1603) song books, in Dowland's own setting for vocal quartet. The lute part, which appears under the solo line in the original publication, is not reprinted here.

feare, Shew mee some ground where

feare, Shew mee some ground where I

feare, twixt hope and feare, Shew mee some ground where

p Shew mee some ground where

I may firme- ly stand, Or sure- ly fall,

may firme- ly stand, Or sure- ly fall, or sure- ly

I may firme- ly stand, or sure-ly fall, or fall, or sure-ly

I may firme- ly stand, Or sure- ly fall, or sure- ly

f I care not which ap- peare,

fall, *f* I care not which ap- peare, So

fall, *f* I care not which ap- peare, I

fall, *f* I care not which ap- peare, So

150

151

TOSSE NOT MY SOULE

VERSE II

Take mee *Assurance* to thy blissfull holde,
Or thou *Despaire* unto thy darkest Cell,
Each hath full rest, the one in joyes enrolde,
Th'other, in that hee feares no more, is well:
When once of ill the uttermost is knowne,
The strength of sorrow quite is overthrowne.

WHAT IF I NEVER SPEEDE

JOHN DOWLAND

live my deare de- ^plight. Come, come, come,

de- light. ^pCome, come, come, while I

de- light. ^pCome, come, come, while

de- light. ^pCome, come, come, while I

while I have a heart to de- sire thee. Come, come, come,

-have a heart to__ de-sire thee. Come, come,

__I have a heart to de- sire__ thee. Come, come,

have a heart to de- sire thee. Come, come,

^{mf} for ei- ther I will love or ad- mire thee.

for ^{mf} ei- ther I will love or ad-mire thee.

for ^{mf} ei- ther I will love or ad- mire thee.

for ^{mf} ei- ther I will love or ad- mire thee.

VERSE II

Oft have I dream'd of joy
   yet I never felt the sweete,
But tired with annoy,
   my griefs each other greete.
Oft have I left my hope,
   as a wretch by fate forlorne,
But Love aims at one scope,
   and lost will stil returne:
He that once loves with a true desire
   never can depart,
For *Cupid* is the king of every hart.
   Come, come &c.

THUS SAITH MY CLORIS BRIGHT

JOHN WILBYE (1574-1638)

It is a pity that so little of Wilbye's music survives, because his two books of madrigals and a handful of sacred pieces reveal him as a most sensitive musician. While he was completely caught up in the current Italian vogue, his use of that style rises above mere imitation: such devices as word-painting and sequence are never employed for their own sake. The two pieces included here are from his first set of madrigals (1598), published while Wilbye was employed as household musician to the family of Sir Thomas Kytson.

wot not what, and O___ I wot not

wot not what, and O I wot not___

wot not what, and O I wot___ not

wot not what, and O I wot___ not

what, And comes and goes a-gaine, I. wot not___whith-er, and

what, And comes and goes a- gaine, I wot not whith- er, and

what, And comes and goes a- gaine, I wot not whith- er,___

what, And comes and goes a- gaine, I wot not whith- er, and

comes and goes a- gaine, I wot not___ whith- er, No, no, these

comes and goes a- gaine, I wot not whith- er, No, no, these

___ and comes and goes a- gaine, I wot not whith-er,

comes and goes a- gaine, I wot not whith- er, No, no, these

160

ALAS, WHAT HOPE OF SPEEDING

JOHN WILBYE

joy hope and joy my treas- ure, Of hope and joy, of

hope and joy, ____ my treas- - - ure, of hope and

joy my treas- ure, my treas- - ure, of hope and joy my

hope and joy my treas- ure, of hope and

hope and joy____ my treas- ure, By de- ceipt to be- reave me,

joy my treas- ure, By de- ceipt, to be- reave me,

treas- ure, my treas- ure, By de- ceipt, to be-

joy my treas- ure, By de- ceipt, to be-

to be- reave me, by de- ceipt to be- reave me, to be- reave

by de- ceipt, to be- reave me, by de- ceipt to be-

reave ____ me, by de- ceipt ____ to be- reave

reave me, by de- ceipt to be- reave

TAN TA RA RAN TAN TANT

THOMAS WEELKES (*c.* 1575-1623)

Tan ta ra and the lament on the death of Morley are from Weelkes'
Ayeres or Phantasticke Spirites (1608). This was the last of four volumes
of secular music published during the lifetime of this excellent composer.
He held the position of organist-composer at Chichester Cathedral and
wrote extensively for the Service, though very little of this music has
survived in complete form. Weelkes was strongly influenced by the Italians
and he often used chromatic devices and harmonies that were quite ex-
treme by English standards. The two pieces which follow show him in
both his lightest and most serious moods.

bloud-y ram- pier, p fa la fa la fa la,

bloud-y ram- pier, p fa la fa la fa

bloud-y ram- pier, p fa la fa la fa

fa la cries Ve- nus in a cham- ber,

la, cries Ve- nus in a cham- ber,

la, cries Ve- nus in a cham- ber,

playfully

mf too- dle loo- dle, too- dle loo- dle loo, cryes Pan that Cuck-

mf too- dle loo- dle, too- dle loo- dle loo, cryes

oo with bels at his shoo and a fid- dle too,

Pan that Cuck- oo with bels at his shoo and a

mf and a

DEATH HATH DEPRIVED MEE

A remembrance of my friend M. Thomas Morley

THOMAS WEELKES

173

WHAT SHALL I PART THUS

GEORGE KIRBYE (*c.* 1570-1634)

Kirbye, one of the lesser-known Madrigalists, wrote almost entirely in the Italian manner. The present piece appears in his only publication, *The First Set of English Madrigalls* (1597). The generally high *tessitura* makes for a very intense vocal sound which is most effective and moving.

*Soprano parts interchange on repeat.

WEEPE FORTH YOUR TEARES,
AND DOE LAMENT

A Mourning Song in memory of Prince Henry

JOHN WARD (*flourished* 1613)

John Ward's *Mourning Song* was one of a number of laments composed for the funeral, in 1612, of the young Prince of Wales, son of King James I. From a contemporary description we learn that the music for the funeral procession was sung by the men and children of the king's chapel accompanied by various instruments. *Weepe forth your teares* appears as the final piece in Ward's only set of madrigals published in 1613. The title page of this collection suggests the use of instruments with the phrase "... Apt both for Viols and Voyces..."

O LORD, INCREASE MY FAITH

ORLANDO GIBBONS (1583-1625)

Gibbons, less influenced by the Italians than his contemporaries, is the continuer of the insular tradition represented by Tallis and Byrd in Tudor times. His writings include a set of five-part madrigals, keyboard pieces, music for viols, and sacred works for the English Service. He became a member of the Chapel Royal in 1605 and was the organist of Westminster Abbey during the last two years of his life. Gibbons' works have great depth and grandeur and are marked with an individuality that sets him apart from the other composers of Jacobean England.

held back

ties. Sweet Je- sus, say A- men, sweet

ties. Sweet Je- sus, say A- men, sweet Je- sus, say A-

ties. Sweet Je- sus, say A- men, sweet

ties. Sweet Je- sus, say A- men, sweet

Je- sus, say A- men, *p* sweet Je- - sus, say A-

men, A- - men, sweet Je- - sus, say A- men,

Je- sus, say A- men,

Je-sus, say A- men,

men, sweet Je- - sus, say A- *pp* men.

sweet Je- sus, say A- men, say A- *pp* men.

p sweet Je- sus, say __ A- men, say __ A- *pp* men.

p sweet Je- sus, say A- men, say __ A- *pp* men.

OKEN LEAVES

A round for three voices

THOMAS RAVENSCROFT (1592?-1635?)

Ravenscroft's *Pammelia* (1609), *Deuteromelia* (1609), and *Mellismata* (1611) exemplify the rarely notated popular music of the sixteenth century. This music gives a picture of Elizabethan life quite different from the elegant one reflected by sophisticated composers of Tudor court and chapel. For these collections Ravenscroft arranged rounds and part-songs with a great variety of texts: sacred, ribald, and nonsense songs, ballads, and street cries. Many of the tunes and texts originate before Elizabeth's reign but remain current, in corrupted form, into the seventeenth century.

*originally a fifth lower

NEW OYSTERS

A round for three voices

THOMAS RAVENSCROFT

*This round is in a mixed meter, alternating between two-quarter and three-quarter time.

O LORD TURNE NOT AWAY THY FACE

A round for four voices

THOMAS RAVENSCROFT

BLOW THY HORNE THOU
JOLLY HUNTER

A round for four voices

THOMAS RAVENSCROFT

1: Blow thy horne thou jol- ly hunt- er, thy hornes for to re- vive a,

2: Shew thy selfe a good hunts- man whilst that thou art a- live a, That

3: man may say and sing with thee, thou hast a mer- ry life a,

4: In pleas- ure all the day, and Ve- nus mate to wife a.

WEE BE THREE POORE MARINERS

THOMAS RAVENSCROFT

spend our lives in jeop- ard- y, whiles ____
we care for those Mer- chant men, which ____

spend our lives in jeop- ard- y, whiles
we care for those Mer- chant men, which

spend our lives in jeop- ard- y, whiles
we care for those Mer- chant men, which

oth- ers live at ease: Shall we goe daunce the
do our states main- tain. To them we daunce this

oth- ers live at ease: Shall we goe daunce the
do our states main- tain. To them we daunce this

oth- ers live at ease: Shall we goe daunce the
do our states main- tain. To them we daunce this

round, the round, the round, and shall we go daunce the
round, a round, a round, to them we daunce this

round, the round, the round, and shall we go daunce the ____
round, a round, a round, to them we daunce this ____

round, the round, the round, and shall we go daunce the
round, a round, a round, to them ____ we daunce this

203

HE THAT WILL AN ALE-HOUSE KEEPE

A round for three voices

THOMAS RAVENSCROFT

REMEMBER O THOU MAN

A Christmas Carroll

THOMAS RAVENSCROFT

REMEMBER O THOU MAN

3.

Remember God's goodnesse
  O thou man, O thou man
Remember God's goodnesse
And his promise made.
Remember God's goodnesse,
How he sent his son doubtlesse
Our sinnes for to redresse,
  be not affraid.

4.

The Angels all did sing,
  O thou man, O thou man,
The Angels all did sing
Upon Shepheards hill.
The Angels all did sing
Praises to our heavenly King,
And peace to man living
  with a good will.

5.

The shepheards amazed was,
 O thou man, O thou man,
The shepheards amazed was
To heare the Angels sing,
The shepheards amazed was
How it should come to passe
That Christ our Messias
 should be our King.

6.

To Bethlem did they goe,
 O thou man, O thou man,
To Bethlem did they go
The shepheards three,
To Bethlem did they goe
To see where it were so or no,
Whether Christ were borne or no
 to set men free.

7.

As the Angels before did say,
 O thou man, O thou man,
As the Angels before did say,
So it came to passe,
As the Angels before did say,
They found a babe where as it lay
In a manger wrapt in hay,
 so poore he was.

8.

In Bethlem he was borne,
 O thou man, O thou man,
In Bethlem he was borne,
For mankind sake,
In Bethlem he was borne
For us that were forlorne,
And therefore tooke no scorne
 our flesh to take.

9.

Give thanks to God alway,
 O thou man, O thou man,
Give thanks to God alway
With heart most joyfully,
Give thanks to God alway,
For this our happy day,
Let all men sing and say
 holy, holy.

NUNC DIMITTIS

THOMAS TOMKINS (1572-1656)

Though he lived past the middle of the seventeenth century, Tomkins' music is very much a part of the late Tudor tradition and shows the influence of his teacher, William Byrd. He has left us a fine book of secular and sacred madrigals (1622), instrumental music—primarily for keyboard—and a large body of liturgical works published posthumously in 1668 as *Musica Deo Sacra*. The *Nunc Dimittis* is from the First Evensong Service in that collection. Our edition does not include the skeletal organ part in the original.

light-en the Gen- tiles, *mf* and to be the glo -

light- en the Gen- tiles, *mf* and to be the glo- ry

light- en the Gen- tiles, *mf* and to be the glo-

light-en the Gen- tiles, *mf* and to be the glo-

held back

ry of thy peo- ple Is- ra- el, *f* of thy

___ of thy peo- ple Is- ra- el, *f* of thy

ry of thy peo- ple Is- ra- el, *f* of thy

ry of thy peo- ple Is- ra- el, *f* of thy

stronger and broad

peo-ple Is- ra- el. Glo- ry be to ___ the Fa- ther

peo- ple Is- ra- el. Glo- ry be to ___ the Fa- ther

peo- ple Is- ra- el. Glo- ry be to ___ the Fa- ther

peo- ple Is- ra- el. Glo- ry be to ___ the Fa- ther

211

INDEXES

TITLE INDEX

COMPOSER INDEX

215

VOCAL PART INDEX

Music for One Voice

Music for Two Voices

Music for Three Voices

Music for Four Voices

Music for Five Voices

Music for Six Voices